GREEN-
COLLAR
CAREERS

GROWING AND EATING GREEN

CAREERS IN FARMING, PRODUCING, AND MARKETING FOOD

By Ruth Owen

CRABTREE
Publishing Company
www.crabtreebooks.com

Crabtree Publishing Company

Author: Ruth Owen
Publishing plan research and development:
 Sean Charlebois, Reagan Miller
 Crabtree Publishing Company
Editors: Mark Sachner, Molly Aloian
Proofreader: Reagan Miller
Editorial director: Kathy Middleton
Photo research: Ruth Owen
Designer: Westgrapix/Tammy West
Production coordinator: Margaret Amy Salter
Production: Kim Richardson
Curriculum adviser: Suzy Gazlay, M.A.
Editorial consultant: James Marten, Ph.D.; Chair, Department
 of History, Marquette University, Milwaukee, Wisconsin

Written, developed, and produced by Water Buffalo Books

Photographs and reproductions
Alamy: Jeff Morgan, Alternative Technology: page 21 (bottom)
AP Photos: page 14
Aroha Organic Goat Cheese: page 40 (bottom left); page 45 (all). Zoë Bradbury:
 page 5 (top); page 5 (bottom right)
Corbis: Alex Hofford: page 10; Kevin Steele: page 11 (bottom); page 12 (bottom); Andrew Lichtenstein: page 15 (top); Howard Davies: page 17 (top);
 Andy Aitchison: page 56
Fairtrade Foundation: page 8; page 48 (left)
Forest Stewardship Council: page 55 (top)
Garden Organic: page 39
Getty Images: Peter Macdiarmid: page 20 (top); Time Life Pictures: page 20 (bottom); Manan Vatsyayana: page 26 (bottom); Melanie Stetson Freeman, The
 Christian Science Monitor: page 42 (bottom); page 44; Jon Furniss: page 50
Green & Black's: page 9 (center right); page 11 (center)
Hippie Chicks Bakery: page 57
Marine Stewardship Council: page 46 (bottom left)
NOAA: page 46 (bottom right); page 47 (all)
Pertwood Organic Farm and Cereal Company: page 7 (center); page 7 (bottom);
 page 22 (bottom); page 37
pomme bébé, Svetla Kibota: page 58 (bottom)
Science Photo Library: page 18 (center); page 27 (top); page 30
Shutterstock: page 1 (all); page 4 (all); pages 4-5 (background); page 5 (bottom
 left); page 6 (bottom left); page 9 (bottom); pages 12-13 (background); page
 13 (top); page 15 (bottom); pages 18-19 (background); page 19 (all); page 21
 (top); page 22-23 (center); page 23 (all); page 24 (all); page 25; page 27 (bottom); pages 28-29 (all); page 33 (top); page 33 (bottom); page 34; page 35
 (all); pages 36-37 (background); page 36; page 38; pages 40-41 (background); page 40 (bottom center); page 41 (bottom left); page 42 (top); page
 52 (all); page 53; page 54 (all); page 55 (bottom all); page 58 (top)
Superstock: pages 6-7 (center); page 9 (center); page 31;
 page 33 (center); page 51
TransFair USA: page 9 (top); page 11 (top); page 48 (bottom right); page 49.
 USDA: page 17 bottom
Wikipedia (public domain): page 16

Library and Archives Canada Cataloguing in Publication

Owen, Ruth, 1967-
 Growing and eating green : careers in farming, producing,
and marketing food / Ruth Owen.

(Green-collar careers)
Includes index.
ISBN 978-0-7787-4853-3 (bound).--ISBN 978-0-7787-4864-9 (pbk.)

 1. Organic farming--Vocational guidance--Juvenile literature.
2. Natural foods industry--Vocational guidance--Juvenile literature.
3. Green movement--Vocational guidance--Juvenile literature. I. Title.
II. Series: Green-collar careers

S605.5.O94 2009   j631.5'84023   C2009-903381-X

Library of Congress Cataloging-in-Publication Data

Owen, Ruth, 1967-
 Growing and eating green : careers in farming, producing, and marketing food / Ruth Owen.
  p. cm. -- (Green-collar careers)
 Includes index.
 ISBN 978-0-7787-4864-9 (pbk. : alk. paper) -- ISBN 978-0-7787-4853-3
(reinforced library binding : alk. paper)
 1. Organic farming--Vocational guidance. 2. Natural foods industry--
Vocational guidance. 3. Green movement--Vocational guidance. I. Title.
II. Title: Careers in farming, producing, and marketing food. III. Series:
Green-collar careers.

S605.5.O94 2009
631.5'84023--dc22
                                                    2009022429

Crabtree Publishing Company

www.crabtreebooks.com   1-800-387-7650

**Published
in Canada
Crabtree Publishing**
616 Welland Ave.
St. Catharines, Ontario
L2M 5V6

**Published in
the United States
Crabtree Publishing**
PMB16A
350 Fifth Ave., Suite 3308
New York, NY 10118

**Published in the
United Kingdom
Crabtree Publishing**
Maritime House
Basin Road North, Hove
BN41 1WR

**Published
in Australia
Crabtree Publishing**
386 Mt. Alexander Rd.
Ascot Vale (Melbourne)
VIC 3032

CONTENTS

Do you ever imagine yourself as a chef creating delicious new recipes? Maybe you dream about spending your days working outside on a farm. Perhaps you enjoy science and would love to be working in a research laboratory. Or maybe you like meeting new people and your perfect job will be helping customers in a busy store or restaurant. If so, you might be considering a career in the food and drink industry.

Each day, millions of people around the world go to work researching, growing, producing, packaging, and selling the food we eat. But what if you want more from your career than just job satisfaction and a paycheck?

Today, many of us want the way we earn our living to reflect the issues that are important to us. We care about our planet. We care about its future. We want to be working "green."

Producing and eating organic food simply makes sense: Organic food tastes better, it is more nutritious and healthful for us, and it is kinder to the soil, livestock, and wild habitats.

Zoë Bradbury works her land with her eco-friendly draft horses, Barney and Maude. Each horse weighs over a ton and has hooves the size of dinner plates!

THE SOIL IS MY CANVAS: ORGANIC FRUIT & VEGETABLE FARMER

I own and operate a farm growing over 60 varieties of fruit, berries, and vegetables. I use a team of draft horses to work my land. All of the farm's produce is sold through our Community Supported Agriculture (CSA) program and to restaurants and local retailers.

I also write about sustainable agriculture and the need for young people to become involved in sustainable agriculture.

At college I studied subjects relating to sustainable agriculture and food systems (systems within a community that integrate the growing, processing, distribution, and consumption of food). After college, I worked on other organic farms for five years before I took the leap and started my own farm. I was 28 when I started my farm.

The challenge for the future will be to not work all the time. There is incredible demand for local food in our area, and we are one of the few farms providing it. It is tempting to get bigger every year, grow more, and hire more help. However, I also want to balance my life with family, adventure, and time at the swimming hole!

Zoë Ida Bradbury
Farmer and writer
Groundswell Farm
Langlois, Oregon

The Greener, Fairer Option

Is protecting the environment, animal welfare, and sustainable farming (the ability to grow the food we need into the future) important to you? Do you think that fair prices should be paid to the people in developing countries who produce food for others to buy and sell throughout the world? If the answer to these questions is YES, then a career working in the organic and fair trade food and drink industry is probably for you.

Zoë Bradbury, Barney, and Maude at work. Many organic farms use horses to power plows and to pull loads around the farm. The horses work alongside the modern-day machinery—lowering the farm's carbon emissions and contributing manure to the crops!

What Does Organic Mean?

Any food or drink labeled with the word "organic" must be produced according to a strict set of standards:

• The use of most chemical fertilizers and pesticides is not allowed on crops or on the soil.

• Organic foods cannot contain Genetically Modified Organisms (GMOs).

• Animals must be raised without the use of growth hormones and antibiotics.

• Animals must be fed natural foods with no animal by-products in feed produced for vegetarian animals.

• Animals must be allowed to free-range—move around outside and get fresh air. If they have to spend time indoors, they must have plenty of space to move around so as not to raise their stress levels.

• Processed foods, such as frozen dinners or other prepared meals that can be heated in the microwave, must not contain artificial additives.

Organically raised chickens must have daily access to pasture where they can behave naturally— eating grass, scratching the soil, and dust-bathing!

Once found only in specialty stores, organic foods and drinks are now mainstream. Many major supermarket chains stock hundreds of organic products.

There's more good news, too. Organic and fair trade food is not only good for our planet. It is also the fastest-growing sector, or area, of the food and drink industry.

An Organic Opportunity

In the past two decades, sales of organic food and drink have grown by 20 percent each year. In 2007, worldwide sales of organic products reached $50 billion, yet the organic sector still only accounts for two percent of the total food and drink produced and consumed around the globe.

This means only one thing for the future—opportunity! We have the opportunity to convert conventional farms (those that are not organic) to chemical-free organic farms. We also have the opportunity to start new businesses and develop new products.

CAREER PROFILE

THE NEXT BIG THING!
MARKETING AN ORGANIC CEREAL BRAND

My job is to market and sell our organic, homegrown range of breakfast cereals. I work with other members of the team to develop new products, I keep the website up to date, and I deal with customer orders and inquiries, press interviews and advertising, and public relations (dealing with questions from consumers).

I love working at trade shows (large exhibitions) where we get the opportunity to showcase our range to dozens of different and potential new customers in one day. My best moment was seeing our packaging and logo in Sainsbury's (a major UK supermarket chain) for the first time!

My future projects will include using our expertise in the adult cereals market to develop a range of organic cereals for children. The new cereals will need names and packaging designs, and we'll need to think up ways to promote the cereals to parents and children—all that will be part of my job!

Tamara Mole
Managing Director/Head of Marketing
Pertwood Organic Cereals
Wiltshire, UK

Pertwood Organic Farm grows oats, barley, and rye for its organic cereals on a 2,000-acre (810-hectare) farm in Wiltshire in the United Kingdom. Pertwood imports dried fruits and other ingredients for its cereals from organic growers around the world.

7

What Does "FAIR TRADE" Mean?

Any product that carries a "fair trade" label has been produced according to the following standards:

• The farmers or producers receive a minimum, and fair, price for their goods.

• Farmers, producers, and their workers must be paid living wages, have safe working conditions, and enjoy freedom of association.

• Exploitative or forced child labor cannot be used.

• Importers purchase directly from fair trade farmer groups, eliminating middlemen. (Middlemen are people or businesses who buy from the producers and then sell to importers, such as large supermarket chains. This extra sale of the product can mean lower profits for the producers and higher prices for the customers.)

• Chemicals and GMOs are banned. Farmers use sustainable farming methods that will improve the soil for the future and protect valuable local ecosystems.

The range of fair trade products is growing fast. It is now possible to buy fair trade fruit and vegetables, coffee, tea, chocolate, ice cream, rice, honey, and wine. This basket carries the mark of the United Kingdom's fair trade organization, the Fairtrade Foundation.

Building Better Futures

Around the world, fair trade organizations are building fair and commercially successful partnerships between growers and producers in developing countries and retailers in wealthier countries such as the United States and United Kingdom. Fair trade food and drink is another fast-growing sector. In 2007, worldwide sales of fair trade products reached about $2.3 billion—a huge, 47 percent increase over sales in 2006.

At the present time, over seven million farmers, workers, and their families benefit from fair trade, but there is still plenty of work to do.

A cocoa farmer cuts a ripe cocoa pod. Inside the pod are the cocoa beans that are used for making chocolate. Since 2003, Green & Black's have planted one million cocoa trees in Belize—that's good for farmers and for the rain forest.

GREEN & BLACK'S—AN ORGANIC SUCCESS STORY

Green & Black's chocolate is a high-quality, organic product that is enjoyed around the world and even stocked in mainstream stores such as Target and Wal-Mart. Green & Black's products are also produced ethically. This means the company pays its cocoa growers fair prices and cares about their working and living conditions. Some of the company's products are fair trade.

Green & Black's was founded in London in 1991 by organic food entrepreneur Craig Sams. Craig had been sent a chocolate sample made from organic cocoa beans. His wife, Josephine—a chocoholic—tried the sample. It was unlike any chocolate she had tried before, and it inspired the couple to start their organic chocolate business. In 1994, Craig and Josephine met with a group of Mayan farmers in Belize. The farmers had planted cocoa trees for another chocolate company. That company withdrew from the deal. Craig and Josephine agreed to buy the farmers' cocoa at a fair price—a business practice that's key to the company's principles. The beans were used to create Green & Black's Maya Gold chocolate—the first product to receive a fair trade mark in the UK.

Caring for the environment is important to Green & Black's. For cartons, the company uses cardboard that is recycled or approved by the FSC (Forest Stewardship Council). It is also researching the use of soya-based biodegradable materials to replace plastic packaging. These materials will decompose if they are buried in landfills (garbage dumps). The company's London headquarters uses video conferencing, recycled paper, and renewable energy sources to cut down on carbon emissions from traveling.

MAYA GOLD™

GREEN &BLACK'S®

ORGANIC

Dark Chocolate
infused with spices and
a twist of orange

55% Cocoa Content

FAIR TRADE CERTIFIED

NET WT. 3.5oz (100g)

Green & Black's wanted a name reminiscent of old-fashioned confectionary companies. They decided on "Green," for the organic status of the product, and "Black" for the intensity of the dark chocolate. This Maya Gold bar carries a label of the United States fair trade organization TransFair USA.

> "Many organic practices simply make sense, regardless of what overall agricultural system is used. Far from being a quaint throwback to an earlier time, organic agriculture is proving to be a serious contender in modern farming and a more environmentally sustainable system over the long term."
>
> David Suzuki, Canadian Science Broadcaster and Environmental Activist

The sale of fair trade products is growing fast around the world. Here, a Starbucks employee in Hong Kong shows the "Cafe Estima Blend" of fair trade coffee sold by the global coffee giant. The growth of fair trade has been driven by consumers asking their favorite stores and coffee shops to stock fair trade products. Shoppers look for fair trade marks on products.

Many more products could be made and sold under fair trade schemes, giving millions of impoverished farmers and workers the chance to work their way out of poverty.

Fair trade food and drink is another industry with a lot of potential—the potential to help others build a better future.

Tomorrow's Food

Today, organic food is produced on small family farms and by huge farm businesses. Organic products can be purchased at the farm itself, at farmers' markets, in specialty stores, and from mainstream, everyday supermarkets. Fair trade products are also sold in supermarkets, in restaurants, and at well-known coffee shop chains.

"Organic" and " fair trade" are terms recognized the world over, with many organic companies now enjoying the same brand awareness, or recognition, as much older and larger non-organic brands.

Above: A worker on a fair trade plantation in India picks tea. Income from fair trade is helping build homes, schools, hospitals, and roads in India. In early 2009, about 14,500 shoppers took part in a fair trade consumer survey across 15 different countries. Almost 75 percent of the shoppers felt that companies should actively support community development in developing countries.

Below: Today, many shoppers are eager to know the "story" behind the food they eat. They want to know where their food was grown and that it was grown in a natural, healthy way. Farmers' markets are a great place for small farmers to tell consumers about their produce.

CAREER PROFILE

KEEPING THE CHOCOLATE FLOWING: HEAD OF SUPPLY CHAIN

My role at Green & Black's is "Head of the Supply Chain." It's my job to ensure that all our products are made, stored, and delivered to customers on time and in perfect condition. I also manage the supply of all our raw ingredients. This involves dealing with 25 different suppliers, ranging from Belizean cocoa growers to Italian chocolate makers, Sicilian almond growers to English dairies. I am generally in the office two to three days a week. I try to spend a fixed amount of time on emails. Otherwise they take over your life! The rest of my time is taken up by meetings: planning company strategy or planning production with suppliers, team management (I have a team of ten) and new product development. Because we supply global markets, we are often on the phone early to Asia and late to the United States and Canada. The rest of my time I am in off-site meetings with suppliers or other business contacts, or traveling. I visit one of our factories in Italy at least once a month. I will usually be in Europe at least one more time per month visiting other suppliers, and I travel to Belize, the Dominican Republic, or the United States every second month.

The best things about my job are working in a dynamic, fast-moving company, being able to make key decisions, and being involved in all aspects of Green & Black's from the cocoa farm to seeing the bars on shop shelves.

Neil La Croix
Head of Supply Chain
Green & Black's
London, UK

Right: Neil La Croix of Green & Black's (center) meets with suppliers in Belize. Neil makes overseas trips to ensure that all aspects of the growing and production process are running smoothly.

Humans have been raising animals as food and planting seeds to grow crops for about 10,000 years. Early farmers worked in harmony with nature. Their animals ate a natural diet of grass and plants. Crops received enough water and sunlight because they were grown with the seasons. Farmers saw how Mother Nature fed plants using animal manure and other decomposing material. In a field where animals graze, it's easy to see how much faster and thicker the grass grows around a pile of manure. Early farmers noticed this natural method of feeding plants and used it for centuries.

A Chemical Revolution

In the 1800s, scientific developments began to change the way people farmed. Scientists developed synthetic, or artificial, substances, such as superphosphates. They discovered these substances could be used to feed plants. Over the next 100 years, with growing populations to feed, people in the farming industry began to believe that artificial fertilizers and pesticides were the way forward.

By the 1940s, the fact that plants are natural organisms that grow and flourish as part of natural systems had been

The synthetic chemical DDT (Dichloro-Diphenyl-Trichloroethane) was first used as a pesticide during World War II to kill mosquitoes and lice on people! After the war, DDT was made available as an agricultural pesticide. Here it is sprayed on crops using a specially designed machine with a seat that raises the driver above the DDT fumes.

This is just a big pile of dung to you and me, but to farmers in the past, and to today's organic farmers, this manure is growing gold! To the plants in a field, this decomposing animal manure is a mixture of essential nutrients—an appetizer, main dish, and delicious dessert!

"Organic farming is rooted in ancient knowledge passed down through generations. Long before science could tell us why certain farming methods would produce greater crop yields, organic farmers were learning the hard way what worked and what didn't—and sharing their knowledge with others."

David Suzuki, Canadian Science Broadcaster and Environmental Activist

all but forgotten by many farmers, particularly in North America and Europe. Crops—which were designed by nature to obtain all the nourishment they needed from the soil—were fed petroleum-based chemicals. Insects, both those that were beneficial (helpful) to the plants and those that were harmful, were killed with large quantities of synthetic poisons.

365 Days of Summer

During the second half of the 20th century, the way people wanted to eat would also change farming practices. No longer satisfied to eat seasonally (eating only the produce grown at certain times of the year), consumers wanted a wide range of fruits and vegetables available to them all year round.

Summer crops were grown during the winter in heated greenhouses, or they were grown in summer, then kept in cold storage for sale during the winter months. Both these practices use large quantities of energy and create carbon emissions.

In addition to the growing of produce at unnatural times of the year, it became possible for fruits and vegetables to be flown from

In 1962, biologist Rachel Carson exposed the damage caused to wildlife by the widespread spraying of DDT in her book *Silent Spring*. Carson highlighted the plight of songbirds that were dying due to DDT poisoning. In her book she described a spring silent of any birdsong. The book caused a public outcry and is often credited with starting the environmental movement.

A field of strawberries in the Salinas Valley, California, in June 1993. A sign on the edge of the field warns people about recent spraying of dangerous pesticides.

YOUR FOOD'S CARBON FOOTPRINT

Food miles—the distance food travels from the field to your plate—have been a hot topic for some time, but they don't tell the whole story of a product's carbon emissions. For example, locally grown food might have lower travel-related carbon emissions, but if the farmer uses chemical pesticides, these are polluting the environment and will have contributed greenhouse gases in their production.

Today, many environmental experts say we should be thinking about a product's "life cycle carbon footprint." A food product's carbon footprint will be a measurement of all the greenhouse gases that were released in connection to that product. To calculate a life cycle carbon footprint we will have to consider: How far has the product traveled? Has it been frozen or kept in storage? Were chemical fertilizers used—the manufacture of which produce greenhouse gases? How much energy was used to make its packaging? Even your shopping trip contributes: Did you walk to a local store to buy the product, or drive several miles in the car to an out-of-town supermarket?

THE LIFE OF A CAGED HEN

Millions of hens spend their lives on intensive egg farms. Here are some disturbing facts about the conditions that these hens must live in:

• They are kept in small cages so that as much of their body's energy as possible goes toward producing eggs. Artificial light is used to trick the hen's body into an unnatural and more productive laying cycle.

• The floor of the cage is wire mesh so waste is easily collected and removed, but the hen cannot scratch the ground (which is natural behavior) and she has nowhere to perch.

• A hen's natural instinct is to lay her eggs in a nest. Caged hens never even see their eggs—they simply disappear on a conveyor belt as soon as they are laid.

• On average, a caged hen produces just 15 more eggs in her lifetime than a hen that is allowed to live a natural life with time spent outdoors.

Rescue organizations are working to find new homes for retiring battery hens. Most hens have had their feathers pecked out by unhappy cage mates. They soon thrive, however, when given a fresh start on organic farms or as pets.

wherever they were grown in the world, at any time of the year—creating more carbon emissions from burning aviation fuel.

Production Line Animals

In the 1950s, many livestock farmers began to use intensive, factory-style methods to raise cattle, pigs, sheep, and poultry. With an eye on low costs and higher profits, farmers aimed to raise more animals, get them to market faster, and use fewer farm workers.

Treated like manufactured products as opposed to living things, animals were forced to breed more often than they would in their natural life cycle. They were given antibiotics to keep them "healthy" and were fed food packed with growth hormones to make them grow fast and, in the case of dairy cows, produce more milk. Factory farms kept large numbers of animals crammed in barns with no time spent outside. Some animals would never see daylight in their lives!

In Europe, vegetarian animals, such as cattle, were even fed commercially manufactured feeds that contained the ground-up bodies of other vegetarian animals, including other cattle! In the late 1980s, this practice came back to haunt the farming industry during the BSE, or "Mad Cow Disease," outbreak in the United Kingdom.

Linked to the feeding of animal by-products to cattle, BSE would lead to the slaughter of millions of animals and the

Hens in cages at an intensive egg farm. A hen enters a "battery farm" cage at 20 weeks old and lives there until she is slaughtered at about 52 weeks old. Each hen has just a small amount of space to move around in—less than a standard sheet of photocopier paper. Food is delivered on a conveyor belt, and eggs are taken away as soon as they are laid.

A cow struggles to get to its feet—a classic BSE (Mad Cow Disease) sympton. During the outbreak of BSE in the United Kingdom in the late 1980s, 179,000 cattle were infected, and 4.4 million cattle were destroyed as a precaution.

MAD COW DISEASE AND vCJD

BSE (Bovine Spongiform Encephalopathy), or "Mad Cow Disease," is a disease in cattle that causes the brain and spinal cord to turn spongy. As the animal's brain deteriorates, it begins to act as if it has gone mad. The disease was spread through the UK cattle population by the inclusion of infected cattle remains in cattle feed. While many parts of the world use soya protein in animal feeds, in Europe it was common practice to use animal remains in the feed of vegetarian livestock.

The first case of BSE was discovered in 1984, but it would be two years before the UK government realized the scale of the problem. By then, infected meat had entered the human food chain.

In 1995, the first case of vCJD (variant Creutzfeldt-Jakob disease), a human form of Mad Cow Disease, was reported. To date over 160 people have died from vCJD. No one knows if there will be more deaths, as the disease's incubation period—the time between exposure to an infection and the first appearance of symptoms—is unknown. There is no known cure for vCJD.

THE LIVING SOIL

In every square foot of healthy soil there are billions of beneficial microorganisms. These microorganisms break down organic matter (dead plants, leaves, the bodies of animals) into a form that can feed plants. The organic matter also improves the soil's structure so that it holds water and is the perfect medium for a plant's roots to take hold. For millions of years, nature managed the soil in this way, and it worked. Adding fertilizers and pesticides to the soil kills soil microorganisms. In the 20th century, many farmers literally killed their soil, turning it into nothing more than a dead material in which to mix up chemicals!

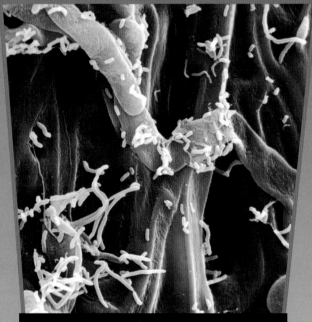

Up to 10 million microorganisms can live in less than half an ounce (14 grams) of soil. This scanning electron microscope image (magnified 2,500 times) shows the microorganism mycorrhiza fungi (the thin yellow strands) living on the roots of a plant. The relationship benefits the fungi and the plant. The plant passes on carbon compounds to the fungi. The fungi processes nutrients in the soil—that the plant cannot access—and passes them to the plant through its roots.

nightmare scenario of the disease spreading to humans through the food chain in 1995.

The Organic Movement Is Born

During the 1930s and 1940s, some forward thinkers began to argue that the widespread use of chemical fertilizers and pesticides was dangerous for human health, wildlife, and the environment. In the decades that followed, campaigners would also fight for better animal welfare standards and would highlight a new concern—sustainability, the fight to conserve and renew the resources we use to produce our food.

The soil on many farms was losing its natural fertility and structure. Fertilizers and pesticides were polluting rivers and other water sources. Farmers were relying on chemicals made from non-renewable fossil fuels to grow the world's food. Conventional farming methods were damaging the planet and using up or destroying precious natural resources. This way of producing food—using up resources faster than they could be renewed or depleting them completely —was not sustainable!

FARMING AND CLIMATE CHANGE

The farming industry is a major producer of carbon dioxide, methane, and nitrous oxide—the harmful greenhouse gases that are causing climate change. Worldwide, conventional farmers are being encouraged to use greener practices, such as the following:

• Biodiesel is fuel made from renewable, environmentally friendly sources, such as oil made from the rapeseed plant. Using biodiesel in farm vehicles can cut carbon dioxide emissions on farms by 50 percent.

• Methane emissions from animal manure can be turned into biogas using special equipment that breaks down the manure with a process called anaerobic digestion. The biogas can be used to make electricity for the farm.

• Nitrous oxide is released when chemical fertilizers are spread on fields. Using fewer chemical fertilizers will reduce the amount of this gas that is released. Some plants, such as red clover and legumes, are very good at removing this gas from the atmosphere and holding it in the soil. Organic farmers sometimes plant these crops in a field one year so that they help "fix" nutritious nitrogen in the field for the following year's cereal or vegetable crop.

Rapeseed is a flowering member of the cabbage plant family. Oil can be made from its seeds. Rapeseed is mostly grown in India, China, and some parts of Europe. Rapeseed oil can be used to make biodiesel. It is a 100 percent renewable fuel source.

Wind turbines are used to generate renewable, "green" electricity. Farmland is a great place to build a wind farm. Some farms set up their own turbines to power their farm and then sell any surplus electricity to a power company.

An intensively reared chicken priced at just £1.99 (about three dollars) for sale in the UK supermarket chain Tesco. This single food item perfectly illustrates the complexities of food production: Consumers want low-cost food; stores compete for customers; farmers use intensive farming methods to cut costs; animals suffer under inhumane living conditions, which can also lead to poorer-quality meat.

A Shared Responsibility

It's easy to portray farmers and the food industry as the "bad guys" when it comes to poor management of our planet's resources, but consumers also play a huge part in the problem. We have all enjoyed a meal of "fresh" summer fruit or salad when there is snow on the ground outside. We don't always question how it is possible to breed, raise, slaughter, package, and deliver a chicken to our dinner table for less than it costs to buy a cup of coffee at Starbucks.

The way we grow, process, sell, and buy our food has become a complex web of many factors: unthinking experimentation; consumer demand; the drive for low costs and big profits; the rise of "pile it high and sell it cheap" supermarkets; bad government policies; and a good-sized dose of "because we could, we did!" The good news is, however, that it's not too late to change direction and set things right.

The Right Time for Change

From those few lone voices in the 1930s and 1940s, the organic movement grew. By the 1980s, determined organic farmers were convincing food stores and eventually supermarkets to stock organic goods. At the same time, consumers were starting to ask questions about what they were eating. The BSE outbreak in the United Kingdom was a terrifying example of what was happening "behind the scenes" in the food industry.

Jerome Rodale (1898—1971) eats seeds from an organically grown sunflower. Rodale was an American writer, publisher, and pioneer of organic food and healthy lifestyles. His company, Rodale Press, launched the magazine *Organic Farming and Gardening* in 1942. Rodale promoted the idea that plants grown in chemical-free soil are healthier

A field of young rice plants.

"We envision a hybrid of my grandfather's and father's farm—fully mechanized and technologically advanced, but less resource intensive, and with a positive impact on the environment. The water that leaves our land needs to be cleaner than when it arrived, the soil needs to be improving every year, and we must share our land and harvests with wildlife."

Greg Massa, Organic rice farmer, California

A LIFE OF WATER, RICE, AND DUCKS! ORGANIC RICE FARMER

Several generations of my family have owned this rice farm, but I never expected to become a farmer. My wife, Raquel, and I trained as biologists (we met in college). We spent several years working in the tropical rainforests of Costa Rica, but we realized we had the chance to do conservation work at home on my family's farm.

We have now turned 100 acres (40 hectares) of the farm over to production of organic brown rice. We use organic manure to feed the soil. At planting time, the fields are flooded, then the rice seeds are dropped onto the fields of water from a crop duster plane. We have installed recirculation systems in the fields to reclaim the water so it can be used again.

It's important that our farm encourages nature and biodiversity. We have planted oak trees along field borders and installed nest boxes for wood ducks, barn owls, American kestrels, and bats. A future project is to create a waterfowl and shorebird habitat in our rice fields.

We sell our rice to restaurants, health food stores, and manufacturers of organic krispy treats. We also sell our rice online and in 2-pound (1-kilogram) bags at farmers' markets. We get to meet our customers, and we make more profit by selling direct to the people who eat our rice.

Greg Massa
Organic rice farmer
California

It's possible to construct buildings using bales of straw for the walls, as shown here. Greg Massa's eco-friendly farmhouse is built from bales of rice straw—the stalks that are left over when the rice is harvested. The straw bale walls are covered with stucco and are so thick that they keep the house cool so Greg does not need to use air-conditioning.

Public opinion began to turn away from anonymous, mass-produced farm products—and toward organic farmers and their produce!

How Is Organic Farming Different?

Organic farming is all about working with nature as opposed to dominating nature with chemicals. Consequently, organic farming practices do not cause pollution. Rather, they are kind to wildlife and wild habitats, and they promote biodiversity.

The key to successful organic farming is healthy soil. Organic farmers feed their soil using moisture-retaining natural materials, such as animal manure and compost. Plants that grow in nutritious, moist soil are stronger and under less stress. Just like a human or animal, a plant living a healthy, stress-free life is better able to fight off disease without the need for artificial chemicals.

Healthy soil is also important to organic livestock farmers. Animals fed on grass and plants grown in nutrient-rich, organic soil are also healthier. Natural preventive methods, such as regularly moving animals to fresh pasture, are also used on organic livestock farms. This stops the build-up of parasites (organisms that live off of nutrition provided by another organism, known as the host) where the animals live. It also eliminates the need for regular doses of drugs and antibiotics.

Before planting oats and barley, a farm worker on Pertwood Organic Farm spreads nutritious organic "muck" on the fields (below). The muck includes cow and chicken manure (top), old straw bales, and leftovers from last year's crops. All these ingredients have been composted (allowed to decompose, or rot).

"Once people find out that, after the last tree has been cut down, the last fish caught, and the last river polluted, money cannot be eaten—hopefully they will change their attitudes and principles."

Jeanne van Kuyk, Organic Goat Farmer, New Zealand

clover
(green manure)

potatoes

onions

carrots

wheat

sheep for manure

pumpkins

lettuce

ORGANIC METHODS CROP ROTATION

Organic farmers use crop rotation to keep soil healthy. Each field is planted with a different crop every year so that diseases or pest infestations that affect a particular crop cannot build up in that field. Also, different crops need different nutrients and take them from different parts of the soil. This means none of the soil's nutrition is wasted.

Sometimes farmers include animals in the rotation. Sheep might be grazed in a field one year, so that they leave behind a generous amount of natural fertilizer for the following year's wheat crop!

An organic farmer growing the eight crops shown here on an eight-year rotation has 5,040 different combinations to choose from to get the best from the crops.

WHAT IS BIODIVERSITY?

Biodiversity is short for "biological diversity." It means every living thing on Earth— every microorganism, plant, insect, animal, and person. Over millions of years, individual species have evolved to live together and depend on each other. Just like the pieces of a huge jigsaw puzzle, every piece needs the others for the picture to be complete. When we poison a species of insect or cut down a forest, it's like taking away a piece of the jigsaw. What today's scientists don't know for sure is how many pieces of our jigsaw we can afford to lose before the whole picture is completely ruined!

WHY EAT ORGANIC FOOD?

• Organic food tastes better: Fruit and vegetable varieties are chosen for their taste and nutritional value rather than for shelf life and appearance. Naturally raised, stress-free animals provide better-tasting meat.

• Organic foods contain more vitamins and minerals.

• Organic food does not contain pesticide residues.

• Organic food is usually fresher—often from the field to your plate in a day. Conventionally farmed produce is sometimes stored for months.

• The organic certification process means the production of the food is carefully monitored and regularly checked.

• Organic growing methods are more labor-intensive than conventional farming. This means more jobs for rural communities.

• Organic farming methods produce low quantities of greenhouse gas emissions and no pollution.

Organic produce for sale at the entrance to a farm. The produce has traveled just a few yards from the field to the point of sale!

A plant naturally produces antioxidants when it is under attack from pests or weeds. Antioxidants also help our bodies fight cancer. If pests are killed off by chemicals, plants stop producing antioxidant substances. Therefore, naturally grown organic fruits and vegetables contain more cancer-fighting antioxidants than do non-organic versions.

Animal welfare is also of prime importance. Organic animals live outdoors, get plenty of fresh air and exercise, and live as natural and stress-free a life as possible.

Making it Official

Before farmers can label their produce "Organic," their land and farm must be certified organic by an official certification body: for example, the United States Department of Agriculture (USDA) in the United States; the Canadian General Standards Board in Canada; or, in the United Kingdom, the Soil Association. To obtain certification, the farmland must be free of chemicals for a period of time, usually three years, and the grower must have comprehensive records giving details of the daily running of the farm and the organic methods used.

The Big Picture

While organic food is now big business and firmly in the mainstream, it's important to remember that 98 percent of the world's food is still grown and produced using non-organic methods. Around the world, chemicals are still sprayed onto crops, animals are made to suffer, and food is produced in a way that cannot be sustained into the future.

The rules of organic certification state that organic farmers must keep detailed records about their animals and the farm. This means organic farmers pay a lot of attention to their animals. Organic farmers say farming is more fun this way as well!

There is also a new food issue causing concern and debate around the world—the creation of Genetically Modified (GM) foods. GM foods are created by grafting desirable genetic material from one organism onto another. This is done to engineer foods with particular traits, or qualities.

Supporters of GM foods say this science will enable us to create plants that are resistant to pests, diseases, and drought. They believe the technology could solve the world's food shortages. Opponents of GM foods believe the technology could be dangerous. They say we cannot know for sure the effect that GM organisms will have on human health or what the long-term effect on other plants and animals will be in any ecosystem where GM plants are grown. As the debate between scientists, GM seed and food companies, and protestors rages on, consumers have become reluctant to accept GM foods, and in many places GM foods are currently banned.

"Let's keep using organic techniques as ammunition against the problem of climate change. Let's be clear: If we want to hit our greenhouse gas targets, we need all the ammunition we can get."

Mariann Fischer Boel,
European Union (EU)
Commissioner for Agriculture

The debate about GM foods has spread around the world. Here activists from the environmental group Greenpeace stage a protest in front of the Agricultural Ministry in New Delhi, India, in June 2006. The activists are demanding investigations into the mysterious deaths of 1,600 sheep and cattle after they grazed in GM cotton fields.

GM—THE ARGUMENTS

• Supporters of GM technology say that humans have been selectively breeding plants and animals to have particular traits since farming began. GM technology is simply a more advanced and direct approach. Opponents say that while selective breeding is nature's way of ensuring survival of the fittest, nature does not mix different species. GM technology, for example, can transfer the genes of Arctic salmon to tomatoes to make them frost resistant.

• GM supporters say that plants can be bred that will tolerate harsh growing conditions in poverty-stricken developing countries. Opponents argue that GM food development is expensive. Poor countries will not be able to develop their own GM seeds and will only benefit if they buy seeds from large corporations in rich countries.

• Since farming began, farmers have collected seed from their crops to plant the following year. GM seed companies engineer their plants to produce sterile seeds that are incapable of producing plants. This means the farmer must buy new seed each year.

• Large GM seed producers are buying smaller companies. Many people are concerned that a handful of powerful companies producing a range of genetically identical seeds soon could control our food supply. What would happen if a new disease were to evolve that those seeds could not resist? Genetic diversity is the best way to ensure fitness and survival—nature shows us this.

Above: Genetically modified soya beans growing in Tennessee. A gene has been introduced to the GM soya that makes it resistant to the herbicide (weedkiller) *Roundup*. A crop of *Roundup Ready* soya can be sprayed with the herbicide without damaging the soya bean plants. Below: This corn has been engineered to be resistant to glyphosinate, a toxic weedkiller. The argument for creating these GM plants: Soya beans and corn are important food crops around the world. The argument against: Should it be made easier for farmers to use toxic chemicals on food?

CHAPTER 3

GROWING GREEN ON AN ORGANIC FARM

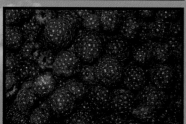

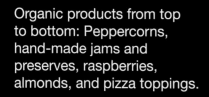

Wheat, oats, potatoes, peaches, tomatoes, apples, olives, oranges, seeds, coriander, almonds, peppercorns, grapes—every type of cereal crop, fruit, vegetables, nuts, herbs, or spices can be grown organically. Many organic growers manufacture an organic product using their crops. Fruit crops become jellies and jams, and grapes are made into organic wine. Some growers sell their crops and produce to manufacturers to become every type of foodstuff imaginable—from organic breakfast cereal to pizza toppings!

Organic Raw Ingredients

The demand for raw ingredients for manufactured organic foods, such as frozen meals, is now outstripping homegrown supply in parts of the world such as the United States, Canada, and the United Kingdom.

A field of organic sunflowers will produce seeds for eating, for use as sunflower oil, or in breakfast cereals, salads, and baked goods.

Organic products from top to bottom: Peppercorns, hand-made jams and preserves, raspberries, almonds, and pizza toppings.

In the United States, about one billion dollars is spent each year on organic ingredients imported from other parts of the world. This trade is important to overseas farmers, but there is an opportunity for U.S. and Canadian growers to supply these ingredients if more farms are certified organic. Less than one percent of the farmland in North America is certified organic. More organic farms in the future will mean more farming jobs.

New Breeds

Every plant-based food grown on a farm begins with a seed. Around the world, organic plant breeders are developing new organic plant varieties. They try to breed new

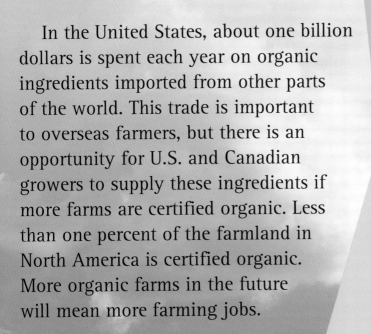

CAREER PROFILE

GREEN GRAPES AND WINE: ORGANIC WINE GROWER AND PRODUCER

We established our organic vineyard in 1993. I had not previously worked in the wine industry, but I had just completed a postgraduate diploma in Viticulture (the science of growing grapes) and Oenology (the science and study of wine making). I had always wanted to get into farming and horticulture, and the wine training seemed a perfect way to make a value-added product from the primary produce. What I regard as my real education, however, began with work experience in vineyards and wineries in New Zealand and as a winemaker in an organic winery near Geneva, Switzerland.

Farming, especially on a small scale, helps develop a very wide range of practical skills. There are always building projects and tractors and equipment to maintain. Marketing and selling the product is never ending-and so is paperwork!

Springtime keeps us busy managing all the new growth in the vineyard, and mowing and weeding. Summer sees us harvesting, and then in autumn and winter wine making becomes the focus inside. We also have to prune the vines, repair trellis structure and wire, and replant or establish new vineyard areas. We sell our wine in the vineyard shop. We also sell wholesale to wine stores, supermarkets, and restaurants.

We would love to see more vineyards become organic and so need plenty of keen young trainees entering the industry

Ian Newton
Owner, Farmer, and Wine Maker
Sunset Valley Vineyard
Nelson, New Zealand

plants that have higher yields of fruit or vegetables. They also breed for improved disease and pest resistance, better flavors, and higher nutritional values.

Plant breeders are part scientist and part grower. Their work involves observing many types of plants to see how well they grow. They then cross-breed plants to create new varieties. For example, perhaps one variety of carrot is very resistant to pests, and another variety has a wonderful taste. The plant breeder will take pollen from the flowers of one plant and, just as insects do in the wild, put it onto the part of the other plant, called the stigma, that receives pollen. When that plant produces seed, the seed is then collected and grown to test if the new plant has both the pest resistance and the flavor.

When a new plant variety is developed, research farms carry out growing trials for several seasons. If the new variety is successful in the trials, it will be grown commercially (in vast quantities) on seed farms. The new plant is given a name, and the seed is sold to farmers and gardeners.

A plant breeder pollinates a potato flower with pollen from another species of potato plant.

"I would say that plant breeding is 25 percent art, 25 percent observation, 25 percent science, and 25 percent luck. There is nothing like getting one of your plant selections approved and seeing the food make its way onto our tables."

Richard Bernard
Organic Plant Breeder

CAREER PROFILE

TOMORROW'S NEW PLANTS: ORGANIC PLANT BREEDER

I studied Plant Biology and Agronomy, then gained training in plant breeding by working as an assistant to a plant breeder in a major seed company.

My favorite days are when I visit a plant nursery to select some new plants for crossing. I have my camera, notebook, and harvesting tools with me. I scan the crop to observe the quality of the field and to identify anything unusual. Then I enter the field and start my selection work. I observe things such as plant habits, the presence of any diseases, colors, flavors, the number of fruits on a plant. I take photos of my best choices, and then it's back to the office to write a report on which plants I've selected, or to plan some crosses or pollination between plants.

Plant breeding work is equally shared between the lab, the greenhouse and the fields. A plant breeder is a grower, a scientist, and an artist. You have to be able to look at plants and imagine how they could be improved. You must be passionate. Be hands-on in the field and always take the environment into consideration—don't just rely on lab science. A good plant breeder listens to what growers and consumers want—they are our customers. You must observe, observe, and observe. Then let your imagination go—with good science in the background.

Richard Bernard
Plant breeder and research manager
Seeds of Change (organic seed company)
Richard works and travels all over the United States

Plant breeding technicians grow and care for new plants that are undergoing growing trials in greenhouses or in fields on seed research farms. They water the plants, check for pests, and monitor and record how well the new plants perform.

Climate change will mean higher temperatures in the future. For northern countries, such as Canada and the UK, and in northern parts of the United States, this could mean the opportunity to grow new types of crops. In the UK, some farmers are already experimenting with Mediterranean crops such as olives, almonds, and apricots. These farmers are supplying their customers with produce that would previously have traveled thousands of miles by air and truck, creating carbon emissions and polluting the atmosphere.

These farmers are taking advantage of climate change and working to stop it at the same time!

The Future is Diverse

Many organic farms specialize, but some grow up to 100 different crops each year. They might grow fruit, vegetables, and herbs alongside crops of flowers for cutting and selling. They will also tend beehives, sell the organic honey, and keep free-range chickens for eggs.

With climate change causing our weather to become more unpredictable, diversification is a good strategy. If one crop fails because of extreme weather—for example, an unusually hot or wet summer—a different type of crop might benefit.

The Career for You

Life on a small organic farm that grows and sells a variety of crops can be busy and varied. Depending on the time of year, a typical week might include working in the greenhouses transplanting seedlings or watering the plants and checking for pests; making compost or spreading it on the fields; weeding the fields by hand and planting green manure crops (crops that are dug back into the soil to feed it); sowing seeds directly onto the field in spring; harvesting produce and collecting seed at the end of the growing season; cleaning the produce; and packing boxes to be delivered to customers.

The tasks are similar if you work on a large organic farm, but you might specialize in just one crop or carry out a particular task. For example, if you are a worker on a large organic farm specializing in cereal crops, your work might involve caring for the fields while other workers take care of the greenhouses. Your tasks would

> "What I love about my job is the freedom, flexibility, beauty. Farming is like painting with the soil as your canvas. I love to do something that is both beautiful and edible, challenging but infinitely rewarding."
>
> Zoë Bradbury,
> Organic Farmer, Oregon

Spring is a busy time on a produce farm, with thousands of seedlings to care for in the greenhouses (above) and young plants to be planted out in the fields (below).

INSECTS AS FRIENDS

Sometimes organic farmers encourage certain species of insects to visit their crops to naturally eliminate another species. For example, flowering herbs are planted alongside a vegetable crop. Nectar- and pollen-loving insects, such as wasps and ladybugs, are attracted to the flowers and will then make a meal of pests such as caterpillars and aphids that attack the vegetables.

Aphids are tiny insects that suck the sap from plants, weakening and eventually killing them. Aphids are the main prey of ladybugs. Insects that "help" on farms in this way are known as benefical insects.

include spreading tons of organic manure on the fields in spring using a tractor and manure spreader or driving a combine harvester to harvest the crops in late summer. You might be responsible for hundreds of acres of wheat or oats.

How Do I Get into Farming?

If farming is a career that interests you, you can get hands-on experience by working on a farm. Many organic farms need volunteer workers at busy times of the year, such as harvest time.

Some farms also offer internships: You will work on a farm for several months (perhaps during your summer break) doing all the day-to-day jobs while learning about every facet of the farm from the farmer. Sometimes interns are offered food and housing on the farm and will receive a small salary.

Many farmers learn on the job. They start work as an apprentice or general farm laborer and build up their knowledge and experience.

Alternatively, you can pursue your dream as part of your education at a college or university. You can take courses related to agriculture and animal husbandry (raising and caring for animals). Never forget that farming is a business, so it's also worth considering courses that help with business planning and managing finances.

An intern on an organic farm picks strawberries to fulfill an order for a local restaurant. Whether it's in the pouring rain or when the Sun is beating down, there's always something that needs doing on a farm.

Most organic growers work in harmony with the seasons. They grow at the time of year when a crop will naturally be at its best. Vegetable boxes contain different produce as the seasons change.

WHAT ARE ORGANIC VEG BOXES?

Just that! A box of organic produce, often freshly picked that day, delivered to your door. For many small organic farms, this type of "box scheme" is a great way to build a following of loyal customers. Each week, the customer receives a mixed box of fruits and vegetables. Some mixed-crop organic farms make up and deliver their own boxes. Other farms supply whatever crops they have to a veg box company that then makes up boxes with produce from a number of small farms.

SELL, SELL, SELL!

If you want to become an organic farmer, you will need to be a sales and marketing person, too. Many new farmers start out selling their produce at farmers' markets. Rent a stall for the day, tell customers about your farm, and let them sample some of your fruit or vegetables. Make appointments to meet with the chef in local restaurants or the produce buyer at local stores. Tell them how you grow your produce and give them samples to test and try out in their kitchen or store. Make sure the name of your farm is on every box of produce you deliver—that's marketing!

Farmers' markets are a chance for farmers to set out their produce to look like a work of art! Farm volunteers and interns often get to help out at markets—it's a great way to learn about selling.

Starting Your Own Farm

The organic revolution means there has never been a better time for people to start new farms. Consumers are eager to seek out and support small, local growers. The farming industry also needs young people. The drive to use chemicals, machinery, and intensive, factory-farming methods wasn't just bad for the environment and the animals—it was also bad for jobs. Thousands of acres of crops could be grown with very little hands-on work. Hundreds, or even thousands, of animals could be cared for by just two farm workers if the animals were in pens inside a barn with machines automatically delivering their feed. Jobs were lost, and the work of a farmer also became less interesting. For that reason, there has been a

Natural, tangled hedgerows and trees around fields give birds places to hide and roost. In return, birds help the farmer by eating insect pests.

Many farmers cut down trees and hedges on their land to make the land easier to farm with large machines. Conventional farmers who are now going organic are replanting trees and hedgerows. This creates wildlife habitats, and the plants naturally absorb harmful carbon dioxide from the air.

gradual decline in the number of young people becoming farmers. In the United States, the average age of farmers is currently 55 years!

Today, farming organizations are setting up innovative projects to help new farmers. For example, new farmers are teaming up with retiring farmers who have land and farm businesses to sell. Banks and farming organizations are also working to help new farmers obtain start-up loans.

"Organic farming is a growth industry. I would like to see cultural support and celebration for young people who choose farming as a career. I want farmers to be seen in the same respected light as doctors and firefighters."

Zoë Bradbury, Organic Farmer, Oregon

CAREER PROFILE

LIFE ON THE LAND: ARABLE FARM CONTRACTOR

I work as an agricultural contractor. Farmers employ me to carry out work in their fields such as plowing, cutting hay, and sowing seeds. I took a college course in general agriculture and then I took a job on a local farm and got several years' experience before starting my own contracting business. In the past couple of weeks I've been working every day on an organic cereal farm. I've been plowing and sowing spring barley and oats. I use my tractor with a plow or a harrow attached, depending on the task. We've planted 500 acres (200 hectares) of crops. In the summer, I can be working up to 100 hours per week.

You can earn a good living contracting, but the machinery you need is expensive. If you have lots of practical experience, though, you can try to get a business loan from a bank to buy your machinery. That's what I did.

I enjoy being outdoors in all kinds of weather and being able to appreciate the beautiful countryside and wildlife in the area.

Andrew Fraser
Self-employed agricultural contractor
Wiltshire, UK

You don't have to come from a farming background to start your own farm. Many organic farmers are people who made the decision to become organic farmers because they felt passionate about issues concerning the environment and "working green" to help sustain the planet's natural resources.

If you attend a school that has a career adviser, you can discuss your plans with him or her. You might also talk this over with a guidance counselor or check out the vast network of organic farming organizations online. See page 62 of this book for Web sites to get you started.

Young organic farmer Zoë Bradbury has this advice: "Try it first. Work on a few farms. Get dirty. Experience the long hours and sore back. Make sure farming makes you hum. If it does, take advantage of every opportunity, resource, business planning tool, and beginning farmer program there is to help you succeed."

Many organic farms set up wildlife projects and welcome visits from schools and families. You could find yourself digging a pond one day and teaching preschoolers about organic vegetables the next!

Passing on Green Knowledge

Some people with organic farming experience are using their knowledge to help farmers in developing countries. NGOs (Non-Governmental Organizations) and charities train farmers in organic growing methods and

animal husbandry. They also work with them to farm more sustainably. The farmers and their families have more nutritious food to eat and healthier farms. Organic methods improve dry, poor-quality soil, while the money saved on chemical fertilizers and pesticides can be used to buy better-quality seeds.

These farmers are able to obtain organic certification that helps them export their produce. With demand for organic produce in North America and parts of Europe outpacing the amount that can be produced in these countries, there is a huge opportunity for farmers in developing countries to benefit from the organic food boom.

Urban farmers in Cuba learn how to improve their soil and grow sustainably and organically as part of a program created by Garden Organic in the United Kingdom.

CAREER PROFILE

HELPING OVERSEAS FARMERS GO GREEN: INTERNATIONAL PROGRAM MANAGER

I manage an information and advice service for smallholder farmers in developing countries in Africa, Asia, and Latin America. Everything we do is related to the research and promotion of organic farming. I also manage projects that we set up overseas to support more sustainable land management.

Originally, I had wanted to do a degree in agriculture, but this required a year's farm experience. At that time, taking one year out seemed far too long, so I got a degree in Rural Environment Studies. I then studied Land and Water Management. This route was actually useful, because understanding ecological and environmental processes is key to agriculture. Also, I was not indoctrinated (taught a particular viewpoint) by industrialized farming courses.

The money to run Garden Organic's projects comes from government funds, or trusts and donations. Therefore, much of my day is spent raising money. Occasionally, I go overseas if one of our projects has the funds to support this. My trip may be to scope out a possible new project or to monitor an ongoing project and give feedback to the donors. In the last year I've been to Cuba and Uganda, as well as conferences in Italy and Germany and traveling all over the UK giving talks.

I enjoy the freedom of coming up with ideas and then putting them into practice. I get satisfaction from doing something worthwhile. With oil running out, climate change, and food shortages, there is an unprecedented need to support more farmers to grow organically. And it's huge fun!

Julia Wright
International Program Manager
Garden Organic
Warwickshire, UK

CHAPTER 4

ORGANIC LIVESTOCK AND FISH

> "I know of few things that compare to being present at the birth of farm animals. Slaughtering and butchering, the other side of spring as it were, are no more or less powerful. They're just different—and in this difference lies an intense, overpowering sense of responsibility and honor for all life."
>
> Peter V. Fossel
> Organic Farmer

Organic livestock farms follow the same basic organic principles as farms growing crops and produce. There is one big difference, however—your "produce" is a living, breathing animal. With this living, breathing animal comes a world of responsibilities, obligations, and emotions that do not factor into a job in growing crops or turning them into food.

Could You Farm Livestock?

How would you feel about sending that animal to slaughter? Could you cope with urine on your boots? Could you face a giant pile of manure that needs shoveling? How do you think you would feel about bloody births? How does having your daily schedule controlled by feeding and milking animals sound to you?

Livestock animals are raised for three main purposes: Milk (cows, sheep, and goats), meat (cattle, sheep, pigs, and poultry), and eggs (ducks, chickens, and other fowl).

If the answer to these questions is "no problem," then you could be ready for one of the most emotionally rewarding careers there is.

Colleges and universities offer courses in livestock farming, and many small organic livestock farms are eager to offer work experience to volunteers and interns.

Living a Natural Life

Some organic livestock farms specialize in just one type of animal, while others keep a mixture of animals for different purposes. Some organic livestock farms are small, family-run operations, while others are large farms with many workers, all with their own responsibilities.

Organic livestock graze on organically grown grass and plants—the types of food that nature designed them to eat. If they need additional feed, they are only fed vegetarian feeds that are certified organic.

A damaging amount of methane gas is actually caused by livestock flatulence. Organic farming researchers are testing different types of plants and grasses for grazing to see if they reduce the amount of gas being passed by farm animals!

A Sustainable System

The organic livestock farm is a complete system. Healthy soil provides nutritious grass; animals that eat organic grass are healthy; regularly rotating the animals around the farm's pastures prevents the build-up of disease; the animals' manure is used to keep the soil healthy.

This is the essence of sustainability. The farm has everything it needs within its own boundaries to run successfully—and potentially, forever!

Natural Medical Care

Organic livestock farmers prefer to use methods of prevention rather than cure. This means taking care of animals in such a way that they are less likely to get sick or hurt. If an animal does get sick, organic farmers avoid using chemical drugs and antibiotics whenever possible.

Many organic farmers use a holistic approach to caring for their animals. This means they think carefully about every aspect of an animal's well-being at all times—its physical needs, its environment, and even its emotional needs—rather than focusing on symptoms or particular conditions only when the animal gets sick.

Other farmers use medicinal herbs, homeopathic remedies, and

A dairy worker on an organic dairy farm brings in the cows for their afternoon milking. The cows are milked twice a day at 4:00 A.M. and 4:00 P.M., and they are moved to a fresh grazing pasture every 12 hours. An organic livestock farm is running 365 days a year, 24 hours a day.

"The best thing about my career is helping produce food without polluting the world. Organic farming is the single brightest spot in agriculture."

Hubert J. Karreman, VMD,
Organic Dairy Cow Veterinarian, Pennsylvania

even acupuncture. If an animal does not respond to natural treatments, it will not be allowed to suffer but will be given conventional drugs. The animal, and its meat, milk, or eggs, can no longer be certified organic, though.

Organic Dairy Farming

The second-largest organic sector after fruit and vegetables is dairy. Most dairy farmers sell their milk to a dairy company. For example, Horizon Foods in the United States operates its own large dairy farms but also buys milk from about 500 independent organic dairy farms.

Horizon's supplier farms range from tiny operations in which the farmers milk by hand to large farms using computerized milking machines. Horizon sells organic milk and makes organic dairy products such as cream, cheese, yogurt, and ice cream.

Many small dairy farms make their own brands of cheese or yogurt on the farm. Selling a product in its raw state is profitable, but turning it into an unusual

A dairy worker on an organic farm milks the cows. The feeding of synthetically produced growth hormones to increase milk yield is very stressful for a cow's body. Organic dairy cows only give the amount of milk that their body naturally wants to produce.

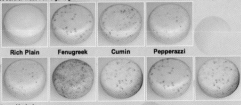
Jeanne at work in the cheese-making room.

CAREER PROFILE

LIVING OUR DREAM: GOAT FARMING AND CHEESEMAKING

We have been involved with animals and farming all our lives. Our goat farm is part of a 100-acre [40-hectare] organic dairy farm. We have 30 goats and we make and sell goat cheese.

I was taught how to make cheese via email by a farmhouse cheesemaker in Holland—the rest was trial and error until I got it right. We sell our cheese from our Web site and we make approximately 25 kilograms [55 pounds] per week.

Our days start at 4:30 A.M. with milk pasteurization, then we milk the girls at 6:00 A.M. Our cheeses are made by hand, and we work on each day's batch of cheese on and off throughout the day. There's another milking at 4:30 P.M. and then admin and emails.

Our life does not make us rich in money terms, but the freedom, and our love for the girls and the land, makes us feel ten times richer than money ever could!

Jeanne and Jan van Kuyk
Owner operators
Aroha Organic Goat Cheese
Waikato, New Zealand

AROHA ORGANIC GOAT CHEESE
Home Cheeses Gallery Our Goats Contact

CHEESES

CERTIFIED ORGANIC
bio gro
NEW ZEALAND

Aroha Organic Goat Cheese is a specialty product with each cheese handcrafted The Old Artisan way, using only methods that are one with nature. It is a round (wheel shaped) firm cheese a bit similar to the famous Dutch Gouda cheese but then made from organic goat milk.

Rich Plain	Fenugreek	Cumin	Pepperazzi

Herbal Experience	Stinging Nettle	Lightning	Nutty Nanny	Tuscany

Click here to order
Goat Cheese Facts   About Our Cheese

AROHA ORGANIC CHEESE: 52 BAILEY RD, TE AROHA - NEW ZEALAND
PH: +64 7 8848555 | FAX: +64 7 8849494 | EMAIL: JJVANKUYK@XTRA.CO.NZ

The internet is a cost-effective way for small farms to promote and sell goods such as cheeses, chutneys, and herbs. Many small farmers market their products by giving background information about the farm and using pictures of their animals on the packaging.

CAREER PROFILE

PROTECTING THE OCEANS: MARINE STEWARDSHIP COUNCIL COMMUNICATIONS OFFICER

The Marine Stewardship Council (MSC) is an international charity that operates a certification program for sustainable seafood. I look after MSC's communications work. This includes talking to journalists, writing press releases, and writing leaflets and material for the Web site. My favorite part of the job is giving live radio or TV interviews. I like to take a complicated "science-y" subject and really stir people's interest in it. I am broadly office-based, but occasionally I visit UK fisheries and restaurants.

I started off in TV following a BSc in Cell Biology and an MSc in Science Communication (explaining science to non-scientists). I worked at the Discovery Channel and also at the BBC as a researcher. I've always been a bit of an environmentalist, so I applied to the UK charity the Woodland Trust for work experience in their press office. I then applied to join the full-time staff and worked there as a public relations officer before joining MSC. To be a press or media person you need to be good at writing—and able to do it quickly. You'll also need to be educated to degree level. The best first step is to volunteer for a charity. Find out what it is like and "get your foot in the door."

James Simpson
MSC Communications Officer
London, UK

Seafood that has been produced in a sustainable way can carry the blue Marine Stewardship Council (MSC) label.

or luxury product is a good business strategy. For example, a locally produced, handmade organic goat cheese will sell for more than the milk used to produce it.

Plenty More Fish in the Sea?

The fish we eat comes from two sources: wild fish, which are caught using small fishing boats or trawlers, and farmed fish, which are bred and raised on fish farms.

Nowhere is sustainability a more immediate problem than in our oceans. Many fish species have been driven to near extinction by overfishing. It's hard to imagine when you consider the vastness of our oceans, but we have simply caught some fish species in such large numbers that they cannot reproduce quickly enough to replenish their numbers!

The biodiversity of the oceans is also damaged by the problem of "bycatch." Commercial fishers may target

A fisher onboard a shrimp trawler in Weeks Bay, Alabama, separates shrimp from bycatch. All the fish seen in the photograph are unwanted and will be thrown back into the ocean, dead.

46

a particular species of fish, but they will also catch other (possibly endangered) species, young fish of the targeted species (which have not yet had a chance to breed), marine mammals (such as dolphins), turtles, and even seabirds. All this "bycatch" is simply thrown back into the ocean—dead!

Fish for the Future

Today's environmentally aware consumers are creating a new market for sustainable seafood that has not damaged marine ecosystems. Many fishers, marine biologists, and seafood companies are now working to identify and then target species of fish, and populations of fish, that have sustainable numbers and reproduction rates and can therefore be fished indefinitely.

Inventors, fishers, and marine scientists are combining engineering skills with an understanding of marine animals to invent fishing gear that reduces the amount of bycatch.

To be viable, the seafood industry of tomorrow must be environmentally friendly and sustainable. In this regard, there is plenty of work to be done!

ORGANIC FISH FARMS

Some fish—for example, salmon, trout, and bass—can be raised on fish farms in large, netted ocean pens. On many conventional fish farms, the pens are too crowded. Pesticides and other chemicals are used in the water to treat disease and pests, and the fish are fed dyes to give them their bright pink color. Waste food, fish waste, and chemicals pollute the surrounding ocean environment.

On organic fish farms, a very limited number of chemicals are allowed and no dyes are used. Fewer fish are kept in each pen to reduce their stress levels, and farms are built in places where fast-flowing ocean currents reduce the buildup of pollution around the farm.

Organic fish farming is still a very new industry—less than a decade old—so it is in the process of developing its organic standards.

About 47,000 endangered turtles were caught by U.S. shrimp trawlers every year before the Turtle Excluder Device (TED) was introduced. Today, up to 90 percent of turtles escape when caught in TEDs.

SAVING THE TURTLES

Commercial shrimp fishers use a process called bottom trawling. A large net is dragged across the ocean floor to scoop up the shrimp. Unfortunately, turtles can become trapped in the nets and, unable to swim to the surface, drown. The Turtle Excluder Device (TED) is a special net designed with an escape hatch for turtles. The World Wildlife Fund (WWF) and other conservation organizations are campaigning for the TED to be used worldwide.

CHAPTER 5

FOOD THAT'S FAIR

Fair trade is a scheme that helps farmers and workers in Africa, Asia, South America, and the Caribbean learn the skills to earn a decent living and compete in the global marketplace. The scheme is run under the guidance of non-profit organizations such as the Fairtrade Foundation in the UK, TransFair USA, and TransFair Canada.

Fair Trade Standards

Minimum prices are guaranteed for products, and farmers are required to farm in sustainable ways. If a product carries a fair trade label, it means its production and all trading relationships associated with the product have met the standards set by the fair trade organization.

A fair trade farmer picks coffee beans (top). About 70 percent of the world's coffee farms are small-scale operations. When you drink a cup of fair trade coffee, you can be sure you are helping disadvantaged independent farmers, not large, wealthy companies.

A coffee crop (right) is planted within a diverse rain forest ecosystem.

Ana and her husband own a small banana farm in El Guabo, Ecuador. Ana is proud of their high-quality fruit, which is grown using environmentally friendly farming methods.

Is Fair Trade Food Organic?

Many fair trade products are certified organic and the growers are paid a premium for these goods. Others, however, are produced using organic methods but are not officially certified because the certification process for many global markets is costly for poor farmers.

Farmer groups are using revenue from their businesses to invest in training for more organic farmers and to help meet the cost of certification. Research shows that consumers also want the fair trade and organic food industries to come together. They want fair trade food to be guaranteed organic, and they want to be sure that organic food has been produced ethically.

Careers in Fair Trade Food

Fair trade organizations employ people with many different skills, but all their employees have one thing in common—a passion for doing good!

FAIR TRADE CHANGING LIVES

In addition to the payment for their goods, farmers are paid a "fair trade premium" to be invested in projects linked to education, healthcare, and other social improvements, such as the following:

• The AGOGA coffee-growing cooperative in Papua New Guinea is investing in a healthcare team for its isolated community.

• In the highlands of Guatemala, the Tzutuhil Mayan people from the La Voz coffee-growing cooperative are sending their children to college for the first time.

• The Sunstar rice-growing cooperative in India is setting up education and healthcare facilities for women and children. They have also built new roads and bridges to reduce the impact of annual flooding.

• The La Riojana wine-producing cooperative in Argentina set up a project to build a reservoir and water tanks and to lay piping to give 400 people access to fresh water.

> "Our workplace culture encourages integrity, innovation, idealism, and impact!"
>
> TransFair USA

Careers might include creating a working relationship between producers and the retailers who stock their goods, finding or developing new products for major store or restaurant chains, or working as part of the certification process ensuring that all the fair trade criteria are being met by producers.

Fair trade organizations also need people with financial, administrative, and computer skills. Whatever your role, you will be working in an organization that shares your ideals.

Fair trade organizations are non-profit charities. They welcome help from volunteers and interns. In return, the volunteers and interns gain valuable experience in this field.

THE INTERNET—YOUR PERFECT JOB?

Today, the Internet is one of the most important tools that any organization or company has for bringing its products or work to the notice of the general public. Fair trade organizations use their online presence to educate people about the problems faced by farmers and growers in developing countries. They use their Web site to promote the products that are available for us to buy, and they give us a fast and focused way to find out what we can do to help.

If you are a creative person with good computer skills, you might consider a career as a Web site officer for an organization that promotes fair trade or organic food. You will need excellent writing skills, a flair for design, and a passion for online communication. You will manage the Web site, produce e-newsletters, and create exciting online ways for the organization to send its message to the world!

You don't have to dress up as a banana to work for a fair trade organization, but it helps! Here, Fairtrade Foundation campaigners raise awareness of fair trade fruit at a music festival in the UK. Thinking up eye-catching promotional campaigns is a vital part of the organization's work. Whether you're the inspiration behind the idea, or the guy in the banana suit, your work will be helping banana growers and their families.

Today, celebrity TV chefs cook amazing meals with fresh, locally obtained ingredients. Cookbooks and magazines encourage us to try home cooking and reject unhealthy convenience foods. Along with the recipes themselves, an interest in the stories behind foods has now sprung up: How was the food grown? Who produced it? Why is it special?

For those interested in the selling of organic food, the career options are growing fast, as organic retailers and restaurants take advantage of this shift in attitudes toward food.

What Can I Get for You?

Whole Foods Market is the biggest organic and natural food supermarket chain in the world. The company owns 260 stores and actively recruits workers who care about food and our planet. Large retail companies such as this offer careers in buying products, in-store customer service, baking, butchery, preparing and selling seafood—the list goes on!

Small, independent organic food stores also offer great opportunities to learn about the

If you want to work in the organic and fair trade food and drink industry and you love people, the energy and excitement of a busy restaurant could be for you.

ORGANIC STRATEGIES IN SUPERMARKETS: BRAND MANAGER

I work for the UK supermarket chain Waitrose. One of my responsibilities is to look after the marketing and selling strategy for all the organic and fair trade products. Part of my job is keeping abreast of current trends and researching and identifying products and market opportunities.

First job of the day is to check emails. Then I check the previous day's sales figures. Tracking and analyzing sales figures helps us keep our finger on the pulse and to react to changes in the market. Then there is the really rewarding and groundbreaking exciting project work where we look at new business opportunities and new products. This might involve looking at consumer trends online to get a feel for how a new brand or product might work for us.

In my job I need to talk to people—a lot! I spend much of my day in conversations with buyers, marketing, design, product developers, and food technologists. I also have a lot of contact with outside NGO's such as the Fairtrade Foundation and the Soil Association.

Andrea Watson
Brand Manager, Waitrose
Bracknell, Berkshire, UK

selling of food. The work will be varied—stacking shelves and cleaning the floors one day, organizing tasting sessions with local producers the next. You will learn about your product range and be able to answer customer questions on food origins or the health benefits of different foods. Your efforts will be going to make a small, environmentally friendly business successful—and who knows, the skills you learn could be put to use in your own store some day!

Life in Green Restaurants
It's a good time to be considering a career in organic catering as consumers become

Supermarket produce buyers must know about the products they are selecting and buying. They must be good at building relationships with suppliers and at negotiating prices.

more enthusiastic about dining out at restaurants offering an organic menu.

As a "front of house" server you will have the chance to be a vital connection between the restaurant's passions and principles and its customers. If you love cooking, you might be considering a career as a chef. Most trainees take a catering course at a college or community college and then gain experience working in restaurants alongside experienced chefs. As a "green chef" you will acquire organic and ethically produced ingredients, have the chance to meet new farmers and producers, and work in a kitchen that saves water, recycles, and composts its food waste!

"We honor the earth by supporting and promoting environmentally responsible products, business practices, and sustainable agriculture."

Outpost Natural Foods co-op,
Milwaukee, Wisconsin

Chefs don't just work in restaurants. You might decide to work for a catering company that prepares organic food for parties and special occasions, such as weddings. You might even start your own catering company!

FOOD COOPERATIVES

One important outlet for organic and fair trade food is cooperative stores, or co-ops. Co-ops are food stores that are owned by local people—sometimes thousands of local people. For example, the Outpost Natural Foods co-ops in Milwaukee, Wisconsin, are a group of stores owned in part by about 13,000 local residents!

The idea behind co-ops is to have a store that supports local farms and producers, sells environmentally friendly organic food, cares for its workers and the local community, supports fair trade products, and gives consumers control of their local food store.

The "owners" pay a small yearly fee, for example $25.00, to be a part owner of the store. They receive a discount and special offers, and some co-ops even ask that their owners get involved by doing some work in the store.

THE DAILY LIFE OF A CHEF . . .

If you like the idea of cooking healthy, organic food for hungry customers, life in a restaurant kitchen could be for you. It's a demanding but exciting career.

• Early morning, and it's time to check in deliveries of fresh meat, fish, and produce. Ordering the best of what's available seasonally is the responsibility of the head chef, or the sous chef (the head chef's second in command).

• The head chef and sous chef will also plan that day's specials.

• The daily inventory must be done. This means checking all the perishable produce and making sure that everything is being used while it is fresh— wasted food will harm your employer's profits!

• With the day's menu planned, the prep cooks must prepare all the ingredients, peeling vegetables and butchering meat in bulk quantities.

• When the ingredients are prepared, the line cooks take over and prepare the section of the menu that they are responsible for that day. In a large restaurant, a line cook on meat and fish may be managing a dozen different cuts of fish and chicken and 20 steaks- all cooking at the same time, and all cooked in different ways!

• With service over, it's time to scrub the kitchen from top to bottom. Then . . . well, it's nearly time to start all over again!

Do you like the idea of experimenting with food? Perhaps you could develop the next top-selling food brand! Think about what foods you like—what would YOU like to eat?

Creating New Recipes

Food manufacturers also employ chefs to create the foods they sell. A "development chef" for an organic chilled-food company will think up new ideas (staying ahead of consumer trends and their company's competitors), develop and test new recipes, and obtain ingredients. The chef will "design" new products that must taste good, be viable for chilling and cooking at home, and be profitable for the company.

It's a mix of cooking, science, and business. Imagine the satisfaction of seeing one of your ideas on supermarket shelves everywhere!

The Forest Stewardship Council (FSC) is an international, non-governmental organization founded to protect the world's forests and to ensure that they are used in a sustainable way. The FSC logo means that wood has come from a forest in which the trees are replaced or allowed to regenerate; the forestry company employs local people and respects their rights to live in and use the forest; and endangered animals and plants in the forest are protected.

GREEN STORES AND RESTAURANTS

Restaurants and stores are eager to be as environmentally friendly as possible! Here are just some of the green measures they are introducing:

- Using eco-friendly cleaning products

- Charging for plastic shopping bags to encourage shoppers to carry reusable alternatives

- Using renewable energy sources, such as solar and wind power

- Using biodiesel in delivery trucks

- Using only recycled or FSC (Forest Stewardship Council) cardboard for take-out food and drink containers

- Using furniture and fittings made from FSC wood

- Recycling and composting food waste

- Using energy-efficient kitchen equipment

- Making staff uniforms out of recycled plastic bottles

- Using organically grown and fair trade flowers for table decorations

Using recyclable packaging and bags, and composting all food scraps and waste (instead of putting them into landfill), are just two ways that all food stores and restaurants can be more eco-friendly.

55

"Securing world food security in light of the impact of climate change may be one of the biggest challenges we face in this century. More than 860 million people in the world today suffer from hunger. Of those, about 830 million live in developing countries, the very countries expected to be most affected by climate change."

Food and Agriculture Organization of the United Nations

The question that many people are now asking is this: Can organic farming offer a solution to global food shortages?

The Future IS Organic

Many poor farmers around the world do not own the land they farm. Organic methods involve long-term investment into the soil—if you might lose your land at any time, is it worth the effort to improve the soil's quality? In many places, the soil is so badly degraded that it will take many, many years to repair the damage. After years of relying on chemicals, people no longer know how

to farm naturally. An investment of time and money is needed to teach the current generation of farmers how to grow organically.

At the end of 2008, a United Nations study concluded that organic farming could be the solution to Africa's food supply problems. In 114 projects, in 24 African countries, yields doubled when organic practices were used in comparison to conventional, chemical-intensive farming methods.

Your World, Your Future

Today we have organic chocolate, wine, baby foods, even pet foods! What's next? If you are an entrepreneurial

Facing page: Members of this family in Uganda have seen their crop yields rise dramatically since they trained in sustainable growing techniques. They are just one of many families in Africa who have received help from the charity called Kulika. This organization trains farmers in sustainable agriculture so that they can go on to train others in their community.

CAREER PROFILE

DELICIOUS, DECADENT, AND GREEN!: ORGANIC SPECIAL OCCASION CAKES

I design and create custom special–occasion and wedding cakes. I have an Associates degree in Baking and Pastry Arts and a Bachelors degree in Food Service Management. When I was in high school, I had a bakery job at an organic farm stand. After college, I worked in bakeries and restaurants using conventional ingredients, but I always knew I wanted to open my own bakery and use organic ingredients as I did at my first job. At the time organic desserts were all brown, heavy as rocks, and tasted awful. I knew it was possible to create wonderful organic desserts that tasted and looked as decadent and delicious as their conventional counterparts. That was how Hippie Chick Bakery was started. I like knowing how much less of an impact my company has on the Earth as compared to others in this industry. My favorite kind of day is when I can create unique cakes with enough time to play around with the many different decorating mediums that I use—for example, fondant, chocolate, and butter cream.

Amy Mastronardi
Owner
Hippie Chick Bakery
Kensington, New Hampshire

Hippie Chick Bakery uses organic and locally obtained ingredients in all its cakes. The bakery recycles, composts, uses alternative energy sources, and bakes with eggs collected from its flock of rescued battery hens.

and creative thinker, perhaps you will set up your own business delivering the NEXT BIG ORGANIC IDEA!

In Ontario, Canada, a group of entreprenuers spotted a gap in the market for organic fast food. They started a business named O zone Organics. From the burgers and fries, to the ice cream and root beer, all the food is organic. The eco-friendly restaurant does not have a drive-thru to reduce carbon emissions. It also uses plates and utensils made from cornstarch, which will decompose in less than 60 days.

By growing, buying, and eating green we are all contributing to a more sustainable world and a healthier future. Being "green" also gives companies a competitive edge with consumers. Being a "green-thinking" prospective employee will give you the competitive edge you need to succeed in tomorrow's food and drink industry.

CAREER PROFIL
ORGANIC FRIES WITH THAT?:
FAST FOOD ENTREPRENEUR

At pomme bébé, we make fre organic baby and toddler food that c be purchased online or from our sh in Newport Beach, California. Our sh has a tasting bar where babies a their parents can test our recip before they buy. I grew up in Bulgar where my family grew their ow vegetables and fruit and home cooki was completely normal. When I w preparing for the arrival of my daugh in California, I looked around a realized that none of the commercia available baby food was fresh or 1 percent natural. None of it was go enough for my child, so I decided make it myself. This was the inspirati for starting pomme bébé—even thou I had no previous experience in t food industry! At the start, I created the recipes myself, cooking in my hor kitchen and holding tasting sessio with my family. Today, a profession chef develops all the pomme bé foods while I concentrate on marketi and growing my busines

Svetla Kibo
Founder and owner, pomme bé
Newport Beach, Californ

Svetla Kibota with her daughter, the very first pomme bébé baby.

t's exciting to have plans and dreams for the future. It's also exciting to try new things. While you wait for school to be over, here are some fun projects to help you find out what you enjoy doing and to whet your appetite for your future career.

GROW AN ORGANIC CROP...

Find out if you enjoy growing organic food. You will be able to buy organic seeds at garden centers in your area. Good plants to choose are lettuce, scallions, and carrots. Most vegetables need to be planted during the spring. It will tell you on the seed packet so make sure you buy your seeds in plenty of time for planting.

Find a small area of ground to use—a piece about 6 feet by 6 feet (1.8 m by 1.8 m) will be plenty. If your family doesn't have a garden, a neighbor might help, or even your school. There may even be a community garden project in your neighborhood.

Dig over the ground and remove any tufts of grass or weeds (unwanted plants).

Your "field" is ready. Follow the planting instructions on the seed packets. Keep the soil moist at all times. You will soon see rows of seedlings appear. Anything that looks different from your seedlings is a weed and must be pulled out so that it doesn't take water and nutrients from your crops.

If an insect pest is nibbling at your plants, find a non-chemical solution by researching online or asking an experienced gardener—farmers use blogs and help from other farmers all the time.

When your crops have grown, ask your friends, family, or neighbors if they would like to sample some fresh, local produce. Think of them as your first "customers" and find out which items are most popular. You can use this information to help you plan future crops!

BE A VOLUNTEER FARMER...

Find out about volunteering on an organic farm in the summer or on weekends. If there are no farms in your area there might be a gardening project or a city farm that needs help. Try Googling the name of your town alongside words such as: *Organic farm, locally grown produce, volunteer gardeners needed.*

Next step—make contact! Perhaps you could visit the farm's booth at your local farmers market, or write them an email: Tell the farmer your name and age and that you are interested in gaining work experience on a farm.

WATCH AN ANIMAL BIRTH...

If you think you might want to work on a livestock farm, try visiting a farm to watch a birth. Many farms have visitor days during the birthing season. It's a great way for you to learn about this part of farming. Most people who watch a real life animal birth say it is one of the most amazing things they've ever seen!

BE AN ORGANIC CHEF...

If you enjoy cooking, try making a snack or even a complete meal for friends or family using ONLY organic and fair trade ingredients. You will need to carefully plan your meal and research what ingredients you need, and where you can buy them locally. Organic chefs need to find all the ingredients they use just from organic suppliers so this is a great challenge for you.

Find out about the ingredients you have chosen. Ask the worker at the store, or the farmer about the food, or read about the product on the packet or on the company's Web site. Tell your dinner guests the "story" behind each of the ingredients in your meal.

BE SMART, BE SAFE!

Please get permission from the adult who cares for you before making trips to new places, or beginning a job in your free-time. Always let them know where you are going and who you are meeting. Check the laws where you live to make sure you are old enough to do a part-time job.

agronomy The science of crop production for food, fuel, feed, and fiber. Agronomy combines various fields of science to study areas such as plant genetics, plant physiology, and soil science

antibiotics Drugs used to treat infections caused by bacteria. Antibiotics either kill the bacteria or keep them from reproducing

antioxidants Substances that work against oxidants. Within the human body, oxidants known as "free radicals" cause cell damage and lead to serious diseases. Antioxidants decrease the destructive power of oxidants and help repair damage. Fruits and vegetable with the darkest colors, such as green leafy vegetables, blueberries, tomatoes, and carrots are high in antioxidants, especially when they are organically grown and eaten raw

artificial additives Non-natural substances added to food for such purposes as making last longer before decaying or brightening its color to make it more attractive to shoppers

biodiesel Fuel made from vegetable oil or animal fat rather than fossil fuels for use in diesel engines

biodiversity The shortened term for "biological diversity." It means the numbers of different species of living things on Earth—microorganisms, animals, humans, and plants

brand name A name given to a product or service to make it recognizable to consumers

carbon dioxide An odorless, colorless gas consisting of two oxygen atoms bonded to a single carbon atom. Carbon dioxide (CO_2) is formed during respiration, decomposition of organic materials, and the burning of fossil fuels. Human-generated CO_2 is a major green-house gas

carbon emissions The release of carbon dioxide, or CO_2, into the atmosphere as a result of burning fossil fuels such as coal and oil. The amount of CO_2 in Earth's atmosphere has been steadily increasing, contributing to climate change and causing harm to plant and animal life

carbon footprint The way in which we measure how much carbon dioxide, or CO_2, a person, a building, or a business is responsible for. For example, each time people go for a ride in a car or use electricity, their activities produce CO_2

climate change A gradual warming of Earth's climate caused by the burning of fossil fuels that give off greenhouse gases and trap too much of the Sun's heat in Earth's atmosphere

Community Supported Agriculture (CSA) A system in which consumers buy local, seasonal food directly from the farmers who produce it. Supporters of CSA pay in advance for a portion of the farmer's crop. The portions they receive reflect how well each type of crop is doing

compost Organic material added to soil to improve its ability to support plant growth. Compost consists of decomposed materials such as plant matter, food waste, or manure. In a garden, materials for composting can be placed in a big heap. Over several months, bacteria, microorganisms, and decomposing animals such as earthworms break the waste down into a soil-like material that can be worked into the soil and used to feed plants

developing countries Nations whose citizens do not yet fully enjoy the standards of "developed" countries in terms of democratic government, industrialization, social programs, and human rights

ecosystem A complete community of living organisms and their non-living surroundings

entrepreneur A person who organizes, starts up, and runs his or her own business

fair trade An organized approach to marketing with a goal of helping growers in developing countries while supporting and promoting fair payment and sustainable growing practices

fertilizer Substances containing plant nutrients that are added to soil or sometimes applied directly to leaves to promote plant and fruit growth

Forest Stewardship Council (FSC) An independent non-governmental, not-for-profit organization promoting responsible management of the world's forests

freedom of association The right for workers to form or join groups of their own choosing, including labor unions

Genetically Modified Organisms (GMOs) Plants, animals, or microorganisms whose genetic structure has been changed for a particular purpose, such as increased nutritional value, faster growth, or resistance to a certain disease or pest

greenhouse gases Gases created by the burning of fossil fuels. These gases cause the Sun's heat to become trapped in Earth's atmosphere—just as the glass of a greenhouse traps heat—and are causing climate change

growth hormones Chemicals that affect the growth of an organism. Sometimes plants or animals are given extra growth hormones to make them grow faster or bigger

microorganisms Tiny living things that are too small to see without a microscope

organic In general, referring to substances based on carbon, which includes all living things. In food production, "organic" refers to food produced entirely naturally and without chemicals

pesticide A chemical (usually human-made) designed to prevent, destroy, or repel pests of any kind. Pesticides include herbicides (plant killers), fungicides (fungus killers), insecticides (insect killers), and any other substances targeting pests

selective breeding The process of selecting certain plants or animals because of particular desirable traits and breeding them to get offspring with those traits

www.massaorganics.com/house.html
Read more about Greg Massa's organic rice farm in California (page 21). Find out about farm life, wildlife projects, and a farmhouse made from rice straw!

www.organicgoatcheese.co.nz/
See an organic farm in action and meet Jeanne van Kuyk's herd of dairy goats (page 45).

www.edibleportland.com/diary_of_a_youn/
Read organic farmer Zoë Bradbury's blog about life on Groundswell Farm (see page 5).

www.icrofs.org/
www.soilassociation.org/
These Web sites are packed with facts and articles about the world of organic farming.

www.benjerry.com/activism/
www.horizonorganic.com/
www.greenandblacks.com/uk/home.html
Find out more about some successful environmentally friendly and organic food brands.

www.gardenorganic.org.uk/international_ programme/
Garden Organic in the UK helps farmers in developing countries go organic (see Julia Wright's career profile on page 39). Find out more about their overseas programs.

www.wwoof.org/
WWOOF (World Wide Opportunities on Organic Farms) is a worldwide network that links volunteers with organic farms around the world.

www.farmers.coop/generation-organic/overview/
www.landstewardshipproject.org/ programs_farmbeginnings.html
www.cfra.org/resources/beginning_farmer
www.nfu.ca/youth/
Information for new farmers: If you think you might be a farmer of the future, these Web sites are packed with advice and information to help new farmers get started!

www.panda.org/what_we_do/how_we_work/ conservation/marine/our_solutions/ sustainable_fishing/
Find out about protecting our oceans and the World Wildlife Fund's campaign for sustainable fishing.

www.smartgear.org/
The WWF runs an annual competition to design fishing gear that eliminates bycatch.

www.msc.org
Find out more about the world of sustainable seafood and the work of the Marine Stewardship Council (see James Simpson's career profile on page 46).

www.gustorganics.com/index.php
If you are interested in the catering industry, read about the world's greenest restaurant—Gustorganics in New York City.

www.transfairusa.org/
http://transfair.ca/en/node
www.fairtrade.org.uk/
Check out these sites for fair trade organizations in the United States, Canada, and the United Kingdom.

ABOUT THE AUTHOR

Ruth Owen has worked in developing, editing, and writing children's books for more than ten years. She writes children's fiction under the name of Dee Phillips, but non-fiction books are her real passion. Ruth particularly enjoys working on books about animals and the natural world. In fact, the first book she can remember buying was when, at the age of six, she saved up to buy *Gorilla Baby*, a book from her school book club that told the story of Patty Cake, a gorilla that was born in the Central Park Zoo in New York. Ruth tries to be as eco-friendly as possible in her everyday life. She loves gardening and grows organic vegetables. Her garden is filled with interesting old junk rescued from landfill! The vegetables and plants receive regular doses of organic manure from Ruth's three pet llamas.

Printed in the USA—CG